ARTISTIC TRICKERY

Artistic Trickery

The Tradition of Trompe L'Oeil Art

Michael Capek

Lerner Publications Company ■ Minneapolis

The text of *Artistic Trickery* is set in Gill Sans type. Trompe l'oeil illustrations on pages 5, 13, 27, 36, 49, and 53 are by Trisha Farrell. Cover design by Darren Erickson.

Cover art: (Left) *Staircase Group* by Charles Willson Peale, 1795, Philadelphia Museum of Art: The George W. Elkins Collection. (Right) Detail from mural, Thunderbird Fire and Safety Equipment Corp., Phoenix, Arizona, by Richard Haas, 1985.

Page one: 1. Barbara Dixon Drewa, *Once I Was the Queen of Diamonds,* 1986. Courtesy of Fischbach Gallery, New York. Page two: 2. René Magritte, *La condition humaine,* 1933. Gift of the Collectors Committee, © 1995 National Gallery of Art, Washington.

LIBRARY OF CONGRESS CATALOGING-IN-PUBLICATION DATA
Capek, Michael.
    Artistic trickery : the tradition of trompe l'oeil art / by
Michael Capek.
      p. cm.
    Includes index.
    ISBN 0-8225-2064-8
    1. Trompe l'oeil painting—Juvenile literature. [1. Trompe
l'oeil painting. 2. Art appreciation.]   I. Title.
ND1390.C37 1994
758'.4—dc20   94-13902
                                  CIP
                                   AC

Manufactured in the United States of America
1 2 3 4 5 6 1/JR 00 99 98 97 96 95

CONTENTS

3. Audrey Flack, *Strawberry Tart Supreme*, 1974.

4. Duane Hanson,
Traveler, 1990.

WHAT IS TROMPE L'OEIL?

When some people think about art, they think of old paintings in stuffy museums. They imagine artists as stern-faced folks who rarely laugh or have any fun. This image isn't true, of course. And the proof is trompe l'oeil.

Trompe l'oeil (pronounced *trump-LOY* or *trawmp-LOY*) is a French phrase that means "to trick or fool the eye"—and that's the whole point. Trompe l'oeil is a way of painting something so perfectly that the viewer is fooled into believing that what he or she sees is *real.*

Trompe l'oeil is different from realism, or still life painting, which tries to represent nonliving objects truthfully. An artist who works in the trompe l'oeil style wants to *deceive* the viewer. The viewer is supposed to think—at least for a minute—that the work is really the object being represented, instead of a painting or sculpture. Trompe l'oeil plays tricks on your visual sense, creating optical illusions. It's a kind of visual game. And the more familiar you become with the game, the more fun it is.

Throughout history, dozens of artistic movements and fads have come and gone. Many different artistic styles and techniques have been used to create trompe l'oeil. Contemporary super-realist artists, for example, whose paintings make us wonder "Is it a photograph or a painting?" are practicing trompe l'oeil.

Ceramic trompe l'oeil jokes have been around since

5. Marilyn Levine, *Black Gloves*, 1987.

people learned how to mold clay, fire it, and paint it to resemble anything from fish to handbags. For instance, when you look at *Black Gloves* (fig. 5) by Marilyn Levine, it's hard to believe they are not an actual pair of worn leather gloves but only cleverly painted ceramic. Even full-sized sculpture deceptions have been created from a variety of materials. Duane Hanson's 1990 sculpture, for example, *Traveler* (fig. 4), is a life-size portrayal of an exhausted tourist.

6. John Clem Clarke,
Construction #14
(Bricks Thru Window),
1976.

Trompe l'oeil murals, which were very popular during the Renaissance, are making a modern comeback on many city walls. Interior designers continue to use them as well.

Artists have chosen to work with trompe l'oeil for a variety of reasons. Maybe painters want to challenge themselves and see how good they really are. Before the invention of the camera, artists used trompe l'oeil to capture events or people in a highly realistic way. Whatever their reasons for doing it, trompe l'oeilists—sometimes called illusionists—all have one thing in common: the desire to surprise.

That's the aim of John Clem Clarke's 1976 trompe l'oeil painting *Construction #14 (Bricks Thru Window)* (fig. 6). The bricks and rough boards aren't there at all. But you almost have to reach out and touch the canvas to convince yourself that it's simply paint.

Marilyn Levine's Ceramic Stories

Marilyn Levine's trompe l'oeil subjects seem sad and worn—things that people might have cared about once but have tossed aside, such as old boots, discarded socks, and battered suitcases. Levine creates these "leather" and "cloth" objects from clay.

Levine was a graduate student in chemistry when she discovered ceramics. When she and her husband moved to Canada in the early 1960s, Marilyn took a ceramics class and became fascinated by the molding and firing of clay. She continued to study ceramics in Canada and the United States, experimenting with various techniques and approaches as she searched for her own unique style.

One day a ceramics teacher gave her an interesting assignment—to create shoes someone might wear to a party. Levine started to work, painstakingly fashioning one shoe. She stood back to admire her work. She noticed that in the time it had taken her to do one shoe, the rest of the class members had completed two.

Worried that the teacher would think she was too slow, she quickly molded two disks like the rubber tips on a pair of crutches. She placed these on both sides of her single ceramic shoe, so it looked like someone with an injured foot had hobbled to the party on crutches. The teacher was as impressed by Marilyn's quick thinking as he was by her skill in creating a realistic shoe.

Later, a friend gave Levine a pair of worn-out work boots. Scuffed, scratched, and battered, the boots had a strange appeal. They told a story. Marilyn tried to recreate the boots in clay, adding even more creases and cuts. This was the beginning of her obsession with making clay objects look like old, cracked leather. Since then, she has created hundreds of these pieces. Each of Levine's painted ceramic objects tells its own story. They create a sense of "history without dates," as the artist says.

7. Marilyn Levine, *Work Boots*, 1983.

8. Fabio Rieti, Whiskas building, Vienna, Austria, 1991.

Artists also use trompe l'oeil for serious reasons. With a little paint and creativity, decorators can turn a blank wall into a doorway or window, or they can make a low ceiling appear to rise to lofty heights. Architects and urban planners sometimes hire artists to decorate plain, unattractive buildings with giant trompe l'oeil murals. The side of the Whiskas cat food company, in Vienna, Austria, is perfectly flat and windowless, but Fabio Rieti's trompe l'oeil mural (fig. 8) makes the building appear curved, with many windows—and a cat in every one.

This book shows you some of the amazing results trompe l'oeil tricksters have achieved over the years. Trompe l'oeil artists have turned their talents to many subjects, from postage stamps to food to musical instruments. Whatever the subject, the overall effect is the same: surprise and delight.

THE FIRST TROMPE L'OEIL ARTISTS

Artists from many different countries have been *tromping* people's *oeils* for centuries. An ancient Roman mosaic floor discovered in a ruin is an early example of trompe l'oeil. The mosaic, sometimes referred to as *The Unswept Floor* (fig. 9), looks like it's covered with the remains of a great feast. There's even a mouse in the lower corner about to start its own feast. Other similar "littered" floors, even older than this one, date back to the second or third century B.C. Evidently the ancient Greeks appreciated the trompe l'oeil game before the Romans.

The Roman writer Pliny the Elder, who lived during the first century A.D., told a story about some of the earliest trompe l'oeil painters. According to Pliny, two Greek artists, Zeuxis and Parrhasios, held a competition to see which of them was the greater painter. Zeuxis's painting of a bunch of grapes was so realistic that birds flew down and tried to eat the fruit. Trying to outdo Zeuxis, Parrhasios presented his painting. Zeuxis eagerly reached out to pull aside the drapery in front of the painting. He was amazed to find no curtain, only a skillful painting of one. Even Zeuxis had to admit he'd been fooled by a better artist.

Pliny goes on to tell how Zeuxis, upset by his defeat, set out to regain his reputation. To his painting of luscious grapes he added the lifelike figure of a child guarding the fruit. Unfortunately, though, when the work was unveiled, birds ignored the child and still tried to attack the grapes.

Similar to Pliny's tale is one concerning *Grandma's Hearthstone*

Mosaics

A mosaic is a decoration on a floor, wall, or ceiling. Mosaics are made from small pieces of colored material that form a picture or pattern. In ancient times, mosaics served as decorative floors, eliminating the need for expensive carpets.

Mosaics are made of small pieces of glass, tile, colored stone, or other hard materials, which are referred to as **tesserae** (TESS-uh-ree). The tesserae are set in a wet plaster or cement base, called the **mastic.** After the mastic dries, a second, thinner coat of mastic is added as a sealer. Then the whole floor mosaic is rubbed and polished for a smooth, durable finish. Early on, people learned how to arrange various colored stones, shells, glass, and even gems to make pleasing pictures. Over the centuries, artists began to create mosaics on walls and ceilings, too. Since people wouldn't be walking on these mosaics, the surface could be left rough, with all sorts of interesting effects. The religious mosaics in the churches and temples of Europe and the Middle East are among the most beautiful works of art ever created.

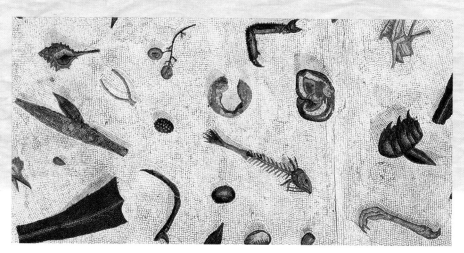

9. Artist unknown, Roman pavement mosaic, date unknown.

(fig. 10), painted in 1890 by the American artist John Haberle. This painting of a cozy fireplace — eight feet tall and five and a half feet wide — was mounted on the wall of a popular Michigan tavern. Over the years, the picture deceived many customers, who pulled chairs up to it trying to get warm. Perhaps they were fooled by the owner's cat, which supposedly curled up in front of the painted fire.

Interior designers still use trompe l'oeil to fool people's eyes. One

10. John Haberle,
Grandma's Hearthstone,
1890.

interior design company (appropriately called Tromploy) came up with its own version of the old littered floor trick. The designers painted a floor with what appears to be a wrinkled scrap of paper lying near the door. Another designer, Charles Goforth, painted a canvas floor cloth (fig. 11) that looks like a beautiful Persian carpet with one corner turned up to reveal some dried leaves.

EYE-FOOLERY

How do the trompe l'oeil artists do it? How do they make us see things that aren't there? That's no mystery. The human brain is easily deceived. When the messages our brain gets from our eyes and other senses are faulty or incomplete, the brain jumps to conclusions, often incorrect ones. For example, you've probably seen a shimmering pool of water in the distance on a sun-scorched highway. Your mind says, "That can't be a mirage!" And have you ever seen crouching animals or hovering ghosts in the shadows of your room at night? When you turned on the light, they suddenly became clothes piled on a chair or blowing curtains.

Every time you go to the movies, too, your brain is tricked. You know, of course, that those moving images on the screen aren't real—in fact, they aren't even really moving. They are still pictures projected onto a screen fast enough that the brain perceives them as moving. In a similar way, your brain's attempts to make sense of things, to put signals in order, make trompe l'oeil work.

For the trick to work, however, trompe l'oeil artists have to follow

11. Charles Goforth, *Kicked Carpet,* 1989.

certain rules of the game. For instance, most trompe l'oeil art depicts inanimate (nonliving), nonmoving objects. It's hard to depict motion in a way that looks real.

Trompe l'oeil artists also tend to portray objects that are flat. That's because it is difficult for any painter to show depth convincingly. We see the world around us in three dimensions. That is, when you look at real things, you can see them from different sides. As you walk around them, the view constantly changes. Of course, that can't happen when you walk by a flat, two-dimensional painting.

It's an old problem for artists—how do you realistically paint three-dimensional objects on a flat surface? The answer is: You can't. Not totally. The successful trompe l'oeil painter relies on a quick effect. After a second or two, the brain discovers the trick.

Another rule of thumb for trompe l'oeil art is that the subjects of the painting should appear exactly the same size as they do in real life. A trompe l'oeil painting of the Eiffel Tower or Mount Everest is impossible. Finally, the objects in a trompe l'oeil painting should not be cut in half by the picture frame. In other words, everything should appear entirely within the frame of the picture (an area that's called the "picture plane") to give the illusion of reality.

Of course, like most rules, these trompe l'oeil rules have been broken freqently, with wonderful results. Even though it's easier to make pictures of still, flat objects look real than three-dimensional or live subjects, that hasn't stopped trompe l'oeil artists from trying. Human and animal subjects have continually turned up in trompe l'oeil art.

The most popular trompe l'oeil subjects are flat items, however, such as mirrors. Other common trompe l'oeil subjects include frames, broken glass, portraits with fake peeling edges or holes, and windows with gorgeous false views.

DAMAGED GOODS

Broken or damaged objects are a favorite subject for trompe l'oeil artists. John Haberle's *Torn in Transit* (fig. 12) is a painting of a landscape—not a very good one—wrapped up for shipment. The package seems to have been torn during shipping, but everything, including the tattered brown paper, labels, and string, is painted.

In *Traité de Paix* (Peace Treaty) (fig. 13) by the French painter Laurent Dabos, assorted papers and pictures, including a rumpled copy of the peace treaty between France and Spain, appear to have slid to the bottom of the frame. The whole mess lies under broken glass—with one dangerously jagged piece pointing right at a picture of the French ruler Napoléon Bonaparte. When Dabos painted this work, in about 1801, the treaty between the two countries had already been shattered, and Europe was on the verge of war. Can you guess who Dabos thought was to blame for the political upheaval?

A Canvas Back (fig. 14) by American illusionist William M. Davis looks like the rough back side of a stretched canvas. A couple of envelopes are stuffed into the frame. Since a *canvasback* is a kind of duck, Davis probably hoped people would be tempted to peek at the wildlife painting they would expect to find on the other side.

13.

14.

The 1894 painting *Time is Money* (fig. 15) by F. Danton Jr. shows a watch and a wad of money hanging on an old cracked wooden door. Part of the trick here is that everything is painted, even the picture's wood frame—except for some of the nail holes, which were punched into the canvas. The artist cleverly painted splinters and shadows around the real holes, though, so it's almost impossible to tell which holes are real and which are only painted. Unless you touch.

13. Laurent Dabos, *Traité de Paix*, c. 1801.

14. William M. Davis, *A Canvas Back*, c. 1870.

15. F. Danton Jr., *Time is Money*, 1894.

Is it a boarded-up window? Something carpenters left behind? No, it's a 1974 oil painting called *Plywood* (fig. 16) by John Clem Clarke. Incredibly, the artist painted every knot, crack, and hole.

16. John Clem Clarke, *Plywood,* 1974.

17. Barbara Dixon Drewa, *Power Inter-rupts*, 1988.

18. Barbara Dixon Drewa, *Pools of Memory*, 1986.

Paintings of paper scraps and other odds and ends tacked to a board or wall is another old trompe l'oeil trick. Early trompe l'oeil artists enjoyed this subject matter, as does the contemporary painter Barbara Dixon Drewa. In her 1988 work *Power Interrupts* (fig. 18), the scorched newspaper clipping tacked to a bulletin board is about the burning of a valuable painting. Drewa may have intended the painting as a protest against people who damage a work of art or attempt to interrupt the flow of creative ideas.

Drewa took the idea of damaged goods to the extreme with her 1986 painting *Pools of Memory* (fig. 17). It looks like a wooden box holding the remnants of a shattered mirror. When you stand in front of the painting, it's as if you are seeing your own fragmented reflection. But *Pools of Memory* is actually a self-portrait of the artist. The reflection in the broken glass is Barbara Drewa's shattered image.

Barbara Dixon Drewa says of her work, "The interval during which a painting is mistaken for the 'real thing' or the 'real thing' for a painting is the triumphal moment of trompe l'oeil art."

MONEY AND STAMPS

Nobody knows where the fad started, exactly, but money has always been one of the favorite deceptions of trompe l'oeil artists. It is said that students of Rembrandt, the famous Dutch artist, used to paint coins on the floor of their studio to see if they could fool the great man into bending down to pick them up.

In the 1800s, the French artist Louis-Léopold Boilly painted a number of objects on the top of a wooden table—including cards, pictures, pieces of broken glass, and some very real-looking coins (fig. 19). Boilly must have laughed to see greedy passersby stop, look, and reach. One of the pictures on the table shows an astonished young man. He's probably meant to mirror the expression of the viewer who tries to grab a handful of those coins.

In the United States during the 1800s, paintings of money became extremely popular. Many works, such as Nicholas Allen Brooks's *Five Dollar Bill and Clipping*, were painted as practical jokes or stunts. Some trompe l'oeil paintings of money were done on a dare. People loved to tell stories of trompe l'oeil paintings of money on tables, countertops, or floors in saloons. Everyone who was in on the joke probably got a big kick out of watching to see who would be tricked into trying to pick up the painted bill or coin.

Painting money realistically was, however—and still is—illegal. The United States government warned trompe l'oeil painters in the 1800s about the possibility of breaking the law. There are accounts—many of them tall tales spread by the artists themselves—of painters being

19. Louis-Léopold Boilly, trompe l'oeil painting on table, date unknown.

arrested because of their lifelike pictures of currency. Some stories claim that the Treasury Department even locked up a few paintings, afraid they'd fall into the hands of counterfeiters.

Treasury agents did for a time suspect illusionist William M. Harnett of counterfeiting. His 1877 rendering, *Still Life—Five Dollar Bill* (fig. 20), was so good that an expert who examined it with a

20. William M. Harnett, *Still Life— Five Dollar Bill* (detail), 1877.

magnifying glass declared it was a real bill pasted to the canvas. Supposedly, the official had to watch Harnett paint another one before he was convinced. Victor Dubreuil painted not just single bills, but piles of it in *Barrels of Money*. Another of his paintings, called *The Safe*, shows a safe crammed full of money. A ticket attached to the safe declares the amount to be almost $500,000. In another of Dubreuil's paintings, the viewer feels caught in the middle of an Old West bank holdup. A man thrusts a gun through the screen of a teller's window while a woman reaches in to grab a handful of money from the drawer. The work is called *Don't Make a Move*.

Stamps, like currency, have been a favorite trompe l'oeil subject because of their flatness. Possibly one of the best (and smallest) trompe l'oeil paintings of a stamp is Jefferson Davis Chalfant's 5-x-7-inch picture *Which is Which?* Around 1890 Chalfant painted a two-cent stamp and pasted a real one next to it. In what seems to be a newspaper clipping glued below the stamps (the clipping is also painted), Chalfant challenged the viewer to guess which stamp is the real one. Over the years, the real stamp has faded, but Chalfant's fake looks as bright and crisp as ever.

FOOD

Most of us love food. Like money, food holds tremendous power over people. Trompe l'oeil artists like to play with our fantasies. They know the attraction of food will make viewers more susceptible to being tricked.

Audrey Flack's 1974 painting *Strawberry Tart Supreme* (fig. 3, page 6) seems so real you can almost taste the sweet chocolate icing, whipped cream, and strawberries. The gray border tells your eyes it's all fake, however. Flack does the same thing with fruit in *Spaced Out Apple*. Painted with slight flaws and looking like they were sliced just minutes ago, the apples and oranges seem to spill right out of the picture.

Of course Audrey Flack wasn't the first artist to depict food in the trompe l'oeil style. In Raphaelle Peale's painting *Still Life with Steak*

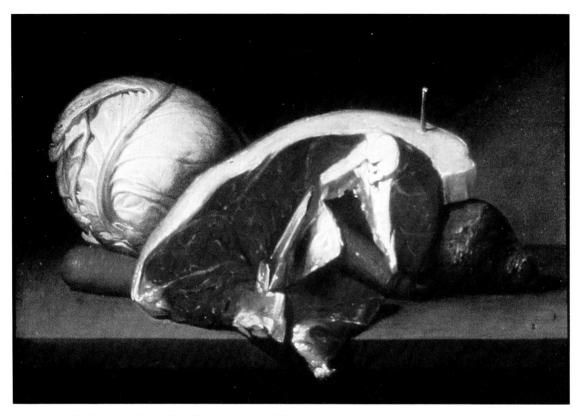

21. Raphaelle Peale, *Still Life with Steak,* c. 1815.

(fig. 21), the raw meat, on a table with green cabbage, a beet, and some carrots, seems ready for the roasting pan.

People have sworn they could smell peanuts while gazing at *Fresh Roasted* by John Haberle. The 1887 painting shows a wooden bin of roasted nuts and a tin measuring can—all behind that common trompe l'oeil device, broken glass. You want to reach out and pick up the peanut that seems to have fallen down to the edge of the bin.

Another kind of food often seen in early trompe l'oeil paintings is not very familiar to most of us today because we buy our food in the

supermarket, already processed and prepackaged. But a century or two ago, dinner might have been an animal scratching in the dirt outside, flying overhead, or hiding in the woods. In those days, it was common to see a rabbit, bird, or fish hanging on the door, waiting to be skinned, plucked, or cleaned. William M. Harnett's 1888 painting *For Sunday's Dinner* (fig. 22) shows a plucked chicken hanging on a pantry door, ready to be cut up for frying.

22. William M. Harnett, *For Sunday's Dinner*, 1888.

A similar painting of game on a door is Alexander Pope's *The Trumpeter Swan* (fig. 23). In 1900, when this painting was done — and before swans were protected as an endangered species — swan meat could be found on menus. Pope was quite concerned about vanishing species and the environment, and he hoped that his painting would be interpreted as a critique of swan-hunting. For many years *The Trumpeter Swan* hung on the walls of the Massachusetts Society for the Prevention of Cruelty to Animals. Perhaps it served as a grim reminder that pictures would be all we'd have left of these beautiful animals unless people stopped killing them.

23. Alexander Pope, *The Trumpeter Swan,* 1900.

PEOPLE

24. Charles Goforth, *Cardinal Borgia*, 1991.

Effective, real-looking trompe l'oeil pictures of people are rare. That's because trompe l'oeil artists usually choose two-dimensional subjects. They also prefer things that are *still*. Since human beings certainly aren't flat and are rarely motionless, tricking viewers into thinking they're seeing a real human being is almost impossible.

But trompe l'oeil artists have tried anyway. Rembrandt is said to have painted a stern, life-size likeness of one of his servants and put it in a window with the aim of "deceiving all passersby." Nobody knows what happened to that painting or whether it really fooled anybody.

Many early mural paintings in Europe portray human figures. A stunning example by Andrea Mantegna is the fabulously decorated ceiling in a room of the Ducal Palace (Palazzo Ducale) in Mantua, Italy (fig. 25). Painted in around 1475, the ceiling shows people (along with some baby angels) who appear to be standing on the roof, peering down through an open dome. Probably nobody was fooled into thinking the people were real. Still, you might get the uneasy feeling of being watched. That's reward enough for a trompe l'oeil artist.

25. Andrea Mantegna, ceiling of the Palazzo Ducale (Camera degli Sposi), Mantua, Italy, c. 1475.

One of the most famous American trompe l'oeil paintings involving people is the life-size *Staircase Group* (fig. 26), done in 1795 by Charles Willson Peale. The painting of a staircase was framed in an actual doorway and exhibited with a real wooden step projecting from the bottom, below the painted steps. On the stairs stand the artist's two young sons, Raphaelle and Titian (both of whom became accomplished artists themselves).

The Peales liked to tell the story of a visiting family friend who, thinking the recently finished painting was a real doorway, paused to greet the boys. That friend was George Washington. Years later, Peale's son Raphaelle painted a famous (non-trompe l'oeil) portrait of President Washington.

26. Charles Willson Peale, *Staircase Group*, 1795.

The Amazing, Artistic Peale Family

Few American families rival Charles Willson Peale's for talent and achievement. Charles taught his 10 children, his brother James, and many nieces and nephews to paint and draw. Charles named five of his sons after famous painters, and three of the sons—Raphaelle, Rembrandt, and Titian—became noted artists themselves. Altogether the Peale family produced at least 20 artists.

Charles Willson Peale (1741–1827) was a man of amazing energy. In the course of his long and active life, he led troops in the Revolutionary War, and he was a saddler, coachmaker, clockmaker, watchmaker, silversmith, inventor, and world-renowned portrait painter. He painted over 1,000 portraits, including several of George Washington and other important people of the day. Peale also established a museum of natural history in Philadelphia.

James Peale (1749–1831), Charles's brother, was known as a fine painter of miniatures—very small portraits or paintings.

Raphaelle Peale (1774–1825), Charles's oldest son, excelled at still life painting. He painted an important trompe l'oeil work known as "After the Bath," or **Venus Rising from the Sea: A Deception** (fig. 27). The figure in the painting appears to be covered by a towel or handkerchief. According to stories of the time, when Raphaelle's wife saw the painting, she tried to pull back the covering to see who was behind it. She was furious when she realized she'd been tricked!

Raphaelle's brother Rembrandt (1778–1860) also studied with his remarkable father, then went to England to study with the painter Benjamin West. Later, in Paris, Rembrandt painted portraits of the foremost scientists and politicians of the day. When he returned to

America, he worked on a portrait of George Washington, which took him nearly 30 years to complete. When it was finally finished, the painting was purchased by the U.S. Senate, where it still hangs.

Finally, Titian (1799–1885) became famous as an explorer and artist. He traveled on expeditions to Florida and into the American frontier, where he was a member of the first party to climb Pikes Peak in the Rocky Mountains. He also explored the South Seas, collecting specimens for scientific study. Everywhere he went, he made sketches of what he saw. In his later years, Titian became interested in the new art of photography.

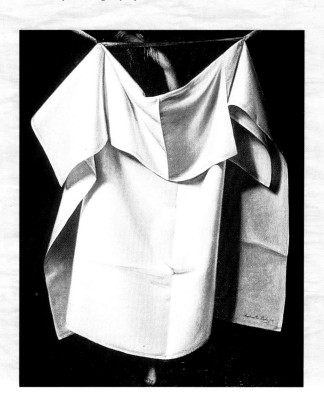

27. Raphaelle Peale, *Venus Rising from the Sea: A Deception,* c. 1822.

ANIMALS AND BUGS

Animals have occasionally been subjects for trompe l'oeil artists. But, again, the problem of making them appear lifelike, even for an instant, is difficult to overcome. At least the mice in Lodewijck Susi's 1619 painting *Still Life* (fig. 28) are a little more realistic than the creature in *The Unswept Floor,* mentioned earlier. Still, it's hard to imagine that an art gallery guard would mistakenly call in an exterminator.

The 19th-century American painter Alexander Pope once painted a lion in a cage, which he exhibited in a fashionable New York hotel behind real iron bars. People from all over the country came to see the convincing illusion. A similar, though much more endearing, picture is Pope's *Pups in Transit* (fig. 29). It shows a crate of four sad-faced puppies. One sleepy pup sticks his nose through the wire. A sign above them reads "For Sale."

29. Alexander Pope, *Pups in Transit*, undated.

30. Tromploy, Inc., faux stone floor, trompe l'oeil fallen plant, 1989.

31. Decorative Arts, Inc., trompe l'oeil mural, 1992.

For people who want pets but don't want the responsibility, modern trompe l'oeil designers have the answer. One company, Decorative Arts, has created a dog that lies peacefully in a corner of a client's house (fig. 31). In a trompe l'oeil floor done by Tromploy, the damage seemingly caused by a guilty-looking cat is fake. The flagstones and shattered plant pot are part of an illusion painted on the linoleum floor (fig. 30). But the cat is real. Just as the photograph was taken, the home owner's pet wandered by!

Insects, because they're smaller, work better than animals in trompe l'oeil. Bugs, especially flies, often sit still for long periods of time. It's easier to make the deceit seem real.

Though it may seem strange, some artists put flies in otherwise serious paintings. For instance, in *Madonna and Child* (fig. 33) by Carlo Crivelli, painted in the 1400s, Mary and the infant Jesus appear to be looking at a fly that has alighted below them on the canvas. Imagine how many museum patrons over the centuries have tried to shoo away that fly. And you've got to wonder what made John Mare—probably the first American trompe l'oeil painter—take the trouble of putting a tiny fly on the shirt cuff in his portrait of John Keteltas.

Some scholars have suggested that these artists had a serious purpose in painting flies. Until the last century or so, people rarely lived past the age of 50. The fly may be a kind of visual symbol. Because flies often hover around dead or rotting things, they are associated with death and disease. Could these flies be the artists' comment on the shortness of life?

Early trompe l'oeil artists also sometimes included skulls in their pictures. For example, the late 17th-century painting *Cabinet of Curiosities* (fig. 32), attributed to Domenico Remps, depicts an old-fashioned collector's case filled with all sorts of things, including a couple of giant beetles. Up on one shelf sits a skull, ominously grinning.

32. Domenico Remps, attributed, *Cabinet of Curiosities,* c. late 17th century.

33. Carlo Crivelli,
Madonna and Child,
c. 15th century.

34. Cy Twombly,
Untitled, 1969.

SLATES AND LETTER RACKS

Still another trompe l'oeil device is a painting made to look like a well-used piece of slate, with old messages and an occasional drawing scrawled on it. A piece of chalk on a string usually hangs in front. Cy Twombly's untitled eight-foot-high canvas (fig. 34) looks exactly like a schoolroom chalkboard, all marked up as though at the end of a busy day.

35. Wallerant Vaillant,
Letter Rack 1658, 1658.

36. Samuel Lewis, *A Deception,* c. 1805-09.

Flat, rectangular letter racks were also good subjects for trompe l'oeil artists. A letter rack was usually a simple board with string, ribbon, or cloth tape stretched tight across it to hold papers down. In earlier times, letter racks were used as a place to stick all sorts of papers: bills, notes, tickets, memos, and pictures.

A good example is *Letter Rack 1658* (fig. 35) by the Flemish painter Wallerant Vaillant. Behind the crisscrossed pieces of tape lie an assortment of letters and notes, as well as a quill pen. What makes the painting so realistic is the careful execution of the rough boards.

Like most rack paintings, *A Deception* (fig. 36) contains various tickets and mementos, even an invitation to President George Washington's birthday ball in 1796. *Deception* was the word used to describe trompe l'oeil paintings before the phrase *trompe l'oeil* began to be used, in the mid- or late 1800s.

Until recently, *A Deception* was thought to be the work of Raphaelle Peale, the oldest boy in Charles Willson Peale's painting *Staircase Group.*

37. John Frederick Peto, *Card Rack with Jack of Hearts*, c. 1895.

In 1986, however, an art historian discovered that the painting was really done by Samuel Lewis. The painting proved to be a double deception!

An American trompe l'oeil specialist, John Frederick Peto, is generally considered the master of the letter rack painting. A picture like his *Card Rack with Jack of Hearts* (fig. 37)—which contains his trademark portrait of Abraham Lincoln—shows Peto's skill at making tattered, worthless items appear interesting and somehow important. Placed against the dark backdrop of what looks like old carved wood, the letters and tickets have a lonely, sad quality, as if the artist wanted to capture memories of happier times.

Barbara Dixon Drewa evokes a similiar spirit in her paintings. Her "letter rack," though, is a cork bulletin board, such as the one in *Once I Was the Queen of Diamonds* (fig. 1, page 1). Among the items stuck on the board is a picture of a 1904 painting by John Frederick Peto—Drewa's tribute to an artist whose work influenced her.

The Sad Fate of John Frederick Peto

Unfortunately, the somber tone of John Peto's work reflected a tragic life. Peto was born in Philadelphia in 1854 and went to art school with William M. Harnett, who became one of the most famous and successful trompe l'oeil artists. Even though trompe l'oeil was at its peak of popularity in the United States during the late 1800s, nobody seemed to like Peto's paintings while he was alive. He died unrecognized and poor in 1907.

Dozens of Peto's best paintings turned up years later—bearing the forged signature of William M. Harnett! An art historian named Alfred Frankenstein discovered the deception, and Peto finally began to get the credit he deserved. Frankenstein found that just after Peto's death, dishonest art dealers had bought most of his unsold paintings and forged Harnett's signature on them.

Old Time Letter Rack (fig. 38) for example, hung in the Museum of Modern Art in New York as a Harnett until 1948. Frankenstein noted the glowing, soft-edged colors of the painting, and the disorderly, aged look of the objects depicted. Since these were qualities he associated with Peto's work, but not Harnett's, Frankenstein took a closer look. He noticed that the letters in the painting were dated 1894—two years after Harnett's death. One of the letters was postmarked in Lerado, Ohio, where Peto was living in 1894. Finally, a museum worker discovered a suspicious patch of newer paint just beside the Harnett signature. When he removed the paint, he found Peto's signature.

Nearly 20 years later, a conservationist who was working with *Old Time Letter Rack* made a discovery that settled the matter once and for all. Stuck to the back of the painting was a second *piece of canvas. When the worker removed it, she found the following inscription:*

OLD TIME LETTER RACK
11.94
John F. Peto
Artist
ISLAND HEIGHTS
N.J.

Now the art world recognizes both Peto and Harnett as leading members of an intense but brief golden age of American trompe l'oeil painting.

38. John Frederick Peto, *Old Time Letter Rack*, 1894.

39. William M. Harnett, *After the Hunt*, 1885.

DOORS

Have you ever seen one of those cartoons on TV where one character draws a phony door on the wall? Someone else comes along, tries to walk through, and smashes flat against the wall. False doors are also a favorite trompe l'oeil subject.

One famous trompe l'oeil door is William M. Harnett's *After the Hunt* (fig. 39). He painted four versions of this picture between 1883 and 1885. The final version of a cabin door is painted with weapons and game killed in the day's hunt. Harnett sold the painting to the owner of a popular New York saloon. The painting was such a hit that soon it seemed like every restaurant and bar in the country wanted a trompe l'oeil door. Dozens of poor imitations turned up, none as good as Harnett's.

But one by Richard LaBarre Goodwin came close. At a fair in 1905, the artist saw the door from the hunting cabin of President Theodore Roosevelt. Goodwin decided to do a painting of the door, with all sorts of things hanging from it, as in Harnett's famous painting. Goodwin displayed his painting in a wooden door frame and even added real iron fixtures and a lock to complete the effect. Some people who saw the finished trompe l'oeil painting wanted to present it to the president as a gift. Oddly, though, it disappeared before that happened, and nobody knows what became of it.

Painted Violin, attributed to the 17th-century painter Jan van der Vaart, is a near-perfect representation of a fine musical instrument hanging on a wooden door. The wood grain in both door and violin shows van der Vaart's remarkable precision.

On the wall behind a Greenwich, Connecticut, bookstore, Anthony Fotia's mural (fig. 40) shows a partially open door carrying the message, "Yes, This is an ENTRANCE." The representation of the door

40. Anthony Fotia, trompe l'oeil mural, 1993.

41. Tromploy, Inc., faux sandstone room, 1987.

and the shop's owner inside is so realistic that people often try to step inside.

Interior designers paint doors and windows where none exist to "open up" rooms. Tromploy artists, for example, created a fancy open window in a client's tiny, windowless bathroom (fig. 41). The window, which offers a view of the country, even has a potted plant that never needs watering.

LANDSCAPES

Have you noticed that in many ways, trompe l'oeil paintings are "more real than real"? That is, an illusionist's work is often so perfect that it could not exist in real life. As the American trompe l'oeilist William M. Harnett said of his art, "In painting from still life I do not closely imitate nature. Many points I leave out and many I add."

That's what an oil painting like René Magritte's *La condition humaine* (fig. 2, page 2) is about. His clever picture shows a landscape painting on an easel that all but disappears before a window with a view of the very same landscape. Magritte seems to be saying, "I can reproduce nature so closely you can't tell the real thing from the fake."

42. Shirley Pettibone,
*Shore at Brighton
Beach,* 1973.

A landscape also appears in Edwin Romanzo Elmer's *Magic Glasses* (fig. 43). The "glasses" refer to a magnifying glass set in a clear glass vase. Reflected in the magnifying glass is a double view—one of them upside down—of a window, through which we can see a lovely woodland view. The effect is magic, indeed.

Magic describes the work of photo-realist Shirley Pettibone, too. Photo-realist paintings are so realistic they look like photographs. Pettibone's 1973 work, *Shore at Brighton Beach* (fig. 42), looks like a color photograph of an ocean beach. It is almost impossible to tell that the painting is not a super-enlarged photograph—until you realize it's *too* perfect. No photograph, no matter how good, contains so much detail and sharpness.

43. Edwin Romanzo Elmer, *Magic Glasses*, 1891.

TROMPE L'OEIL MURALS

From ancient times to the present, people have decorated large wall surfaces with illusionist murals. The word *mural* comes from the French word *mur,* meaning wall. A mural is a large wall painting, although a mural can be painted on a ceiling, too. Murals are often gigantic, covering the whole side of a building or the interior wall of a church. They can either be painted directly onto a wall or painted on some other material, such as canvas or wood, and cemented to a wall.

In the 15th century, muralists and other artists found a new way to realistically represent three dimensions on a flat surface. The Italian architect Filippo Brunelleschi invented a technique called optical or linear perspective.

Linear perspective is the use of mathematically precise lines and angles to create the illusion that things in a painting are receding into the background. Linear perspective is based on the optical illusion that makes parallel lines appear to come together as they move back toward the horizon. The point on the horizon where everything comes together and disappears from view is called the vanishing point.

Using the geometrical approach that Brunelleschi and others perfected, Renaissance artists created many realistic murals. An interesting example from the 1500s is Baldassare Peruzzi's fresco in the Hall of Perspectives in the Villa Farnesina in Rome (fig. 44). Peruzzi blended painted columns and scenery with real architecture—which he designed—so expertly that it's difficult to tell what's painted and what's real. The spectacular view beyond the columns gives visitors the opportunity to step back in time and see the city as it looked in 1515.

Like many early trompe l'oeil murals, Peruzzi's painting has a problem. It's effective only when viewed from one particular spot in the

44. Baldassare Peruzzi, mural in the Villa Farnesina, Rome, Italy, 1515.

room. If the viewer moves, the painting loses its power of illusion. Peruzzi, who was also a designer of stage scenery, probably did not consider this a problem. Most likely, he intended the mural to be seen by dinner guests as they sat at a table in the center of the room, directly across from the mural. From that low angle, everything in the painting looks convincing.

Most modern trompe l'oeil muralists have found ways to avoid the mistakes of the past. Master illusionists use perspective in different ways, by creating several vanishing points instead of just one, for example. Often modern murals are outdoors, too, where the greater distance from mural to viewer can aid the trompe l'oeil effect.

45. Los Angeles Fine Arts Squad: Victor Henderson and Terry Schoonhoven, *Isle of California*, 1971.

A modern mural called *The Isle of California* (fig. 45) by the Los Angeles Fine Arts Squad (Victor Henderson and Terry Schoonhoven), can seem unsettling from a distance. Painted on the side of a San Francisco building, the mural shows the ruins of a building perched atop a mountain of rock jutting from the ocean. Everything about the picture communicates a sense of destruction. The title gives a clue about the meaning of the work. It's supposed to show the future of California, after the big earthquake that scientists say will someday rock the West Coast. To Californians, though, who take earthquakes in stride, the mural is a fun visual joke.

46. Richard Haas, mural (detail), Thunderbird Fire and Safety Equipment Corp., Phoenix, Arizona, 1985.

The modern wizard of walls is undoubtedly Richard Haas, whose sweeping wall murals decorate U.S. cities from coast to coast. Haas's creations are such a familiar part of many cityscapes that hundreds of people pass by them every day—unaware they've been *tromped.*

One of Haas's most interesting works is his decoration of the Thunderbird Fire and Safety Equipment Corporation in Phoenix, Arizona (fig. 46). Starting with nothing more than a bare, concrete box, Haas turned the outside of the building into a 1880s fire station. Through partially open doors, passersby can see fire trucks and equipment.

Haas's 1986 creation of the Fountainebleau Hotel mural (fig. 47) in Miami Beach, Florida, turned a blank wall at the bend of a street into an arch through which the hotel supposedly can be seen in the distance. Motorists would probably be tempted to try to drive right through were it not for the stone wall right in front of the mural.

47. Richard Haas, mural, Fountainebleau Hilton Hotel, Miami Beach, 1986.

Richard Haas, Wizard of Walls

*E*ven as a boy, mural painter Richard Haas loved cities and
buildings. Growing up in Wisconsin in the 1940s, he loved to
make clay models of buildings and draw maps of imaginary
cities. He sometimes drew intricate aerial views of them, including
the particular details of each separate building.

Perhaps the greatest influence on Haas was the presence, just across the river from his home, of Frank Lloyd Wright. Though he never studied with or worked for the famous architect, Richard felt a certain closeness to the man who obviously loved houses and buildings.

After college, Haas tried to find a place in the art world. But he just couldn't seem to develop his own unique style. Abstract expressionism, a style of art popular among young artists at the time, didn't appeal to him. "I never really 'felt it,'" he says of the pictures he created then, "and my paintings seem funny to me now as I look back on them today."

Then he began making dioramas, little boxes with three-dimensional pictures inside and a hole cut in one end to peep through. Inside the dioramas, Haas recreated as realistically as possible the interiors of places he'd read about or visited, such as Frank Lloyd Wright's workshop. He even included people in his miniature scenes. Richard was fascinated by the interplay of light and space in the dioramas. Soon he also began working on extremely detailed drawings and prints of old buildings and houses.

When Haas moved to New York in 1969, he rediscovered his boyhood love of buildings and grand cityscapes. The city's beautiful old buildings inspired him, and he drew them with careful attention. When he was asked to create a trompe l'oeil mural for the side of a building in downtown New York, his career in public art began.

Since then, Haas has created dozens of murals that enliven city walls across the United States and around the world.

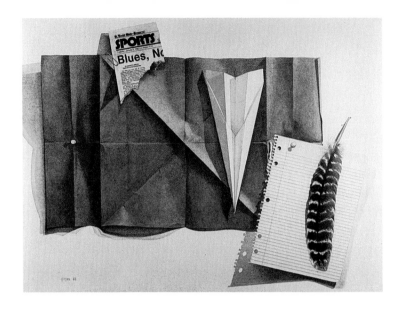

48. Kent Addison, *Still Life #1019*, 1982.

THE TRADITION CONTINUES

Tastes change, styles of art come and go, but trompe l'oeil remains popular. It's no mystery, really. Most of us love things that astonish us, make us shake our heads in wonder, or make us laugh, even at ourselves.

When people see Kent Addison's watercolor paintings, they often ask, "Are those real paper airplanes?" or "Why is a gum wrapper stuck onto that painting?" Of course, those items aren't real. Like so many trompe l'oeil artists before him, Addison likes to paint common objects. His *Still Life #1019* (fig. 48) focuses on paper—torn newsprint, folded brown wrapping paper, and notebook paper. There's also a turkey feather quill, which reminds us of Vaillant's letter rack and the tradition in which Addison works.

The trompe l'oeil game is old, but it remains fresh, and it will continue as long as artists delight in fooling our eyes and teasing our minds. Illusionists will keep on working their magic and making us exclaim, "That can't possibly be a painting!"

GLOSSARY

ceramics • pottery and porcelain; pottery refers to objects made of clay and fired (baked in an oven) at a high temperature

fresco • painting done on plaster while it is still wet

illusionism • the use of artistic techniques such as perspective or shading to give the illusion of reality (the word is also sometimes used to refer to trompe l'oeil painting)

linear perspective • a way of showing depth, or three-dimensional space, on a flat (two-dimensional) surface by using parallel lines that appear to meet at a point on the horizon

mastic • the cement used in making a mosaic

mosaic • a picture or pattern created by cementing small pieces of stone, glass, or other material to a flat surface

mural • a painting on a wall

perspective • the portrayal of depth (three dimensions) on a flat (two-dimensional) surface, such as a canvas. *See also* linear perspective

photo realism • art that is extremely realistic and detailed, like a photograph

picture plane • the surface area (plane) of a painting

realism • a style of art that tries to reproduce reality exactly. (Realism also refers to an artistic movement during the 1800s in which artists rejected the idealization of subjects in favor of accurate portrayal.)

still life • a painting of inanimate (nonliving) objects

super realism • see photo realism

tesserae • the small pieces of glass, stone, marble, metal, or other material used in making a mosaic

trompe l'oeil • from the French expression meaning "to deceive the eye". A style of painting so realistic that the viewer mistakes the painting (or sculpture) for a real object.

vanishing point • in perspective, the point on the horizon line where parallel lines seem to meet and disappear

List of Illustrations and Acknowledgments

1. Barbara Dixon Drewa, *Once I Was the Queen of Diamonds*, 1986. Courtesy of Fischbach Gallery, New York.
2. René Magritte, *La condition humaine*, 1933. Gift of the Collectors Committee, © 1995 National Gallery of Art, Washington.
3. Audrey Flack, *Strawberry Tart Supreme*, © 1974. Allen Memorial Art Museum, Oberlin College; NEA Museum Purchase Plan and Fund for Contemporary Art. © Audrey Flack, 1974.
4. Duane Hanson, *Traveler*, 1990.
5. Marilyn Levine, *Black Gloves*, 1987. Courtesy O.K. Harris Works of Art, New York.
6. John Clem Clarke, *Construction #14 (Bricks Thru Window)*, 1976. Courtesy Louis K. Meisel Gallery, New York.
7. Marilyn Levine, *Work Boots*, 1983. Courtesy O.K. Harris Works of Art, New York.
8. Fabio Rieti, Whiskas building, Vienna, Austria, 1991.
9. Artist unknown, Roman pavement mosaic, date unknown. Scala/Art Resource, New York.
10. John Haberle, *Grandma's Hearthstone*, 1890. © The Detroit Institute of Arts, Gift of C.W. Churchill in memory of his father.
11. Charles Goforth, *Kicked Carpet*, 1989.
12. John Haberle, *Torn in Transit*, 1890-95. Collection of the Brandywine River Museum. Gift of Amanda K. Berls.
13. Laurent Dabos, *Traité de Paix*, c. 1801. Musée Marmottan, Paris.
14. William M. Davis, *A Canvas Back*, c. 1870. The Collection of the Museums at Stony Brook, Gift of Mrs. Beverly Davis, 1953.
15. F. Danton Jr., *Time is Money*, 1894. Wadsworth Atheneum, Hartford. The Ella Gallup Sumner and Mary Catlin Sumner Collection Fund.
16. John Clem Clarke, *Plywood*, 1974. Courtesy Louis K. Meisel Gallery, New York.
17. Barbara Dixon Drewa, *Power Interrupts*, 1988. Courtesy of Fischbach Gallery, New York.
18. Barbara Dixon Drewa, *Pools of Memory*, 1986. West Art and the Law © 1989, West Publishing, Eagan, Minnesota.
19. Louis-Léopold Boilly, trompe l'oeil painting on table, date unknown. Musée Beaux-Arts, Lille, France.
20. William M. Harnett, *Still Life—Five Dollar Bill*, 1877. Philadelphia Museum of Art: Alex Simpson, Jr. Collection.
21. Raphaelle Peale, *Still Life with Steak*, c. 1815. Munson-Williams-Proctor Institute, Museum of Art, Utica, New York, Proctor Collection.
22. William M. Harnett, *For Sunday's Dinner*, 1888. Wilson L. Mead Fund, 1958.296. Photograph © 1995, The Art Institute of Chicago. All Rights Reserved.
23. Alexander Pope, *The Trumpeter Swan*, 1900. The Fine Arts Museums of San Francisco, Museum purchase through gifts from members of the Boards of Trustees, The de Young Museum Society and the Patrons of Art and Music, friends of the Museums and by exchange, Sir Joseph Duveen, 72.28.
24. Charles Goforth, *Cardinal Borgia*, 1991.
25. Andrea Mantegna, ceiling of the Palazzo Ducale (Camera degli Sposi), Mantua, Italy, c. 1475. Scala/Art Resource, New York.
26. Charles Willson Peale, *Staircase Group*, 1795. Philadelphia Museum of Art: The George W. Elkins Collection.
27. Raphaelle Peale, *Venus Rising from the Sea: A Deception*, c. 1822. The Nelson-Atkins Museum of Art, Kansas City, Missouri.
28. Lodewijck Susi, *Still Life*, 1619. The Saint Louis Art Museum/Museum Purchase.
29. Alexander Pope, *Pups in Transit*, undated. Courtesy of Lendy Firestone Brown.
30. Tromploy, Inc., faux stone floor, trompe l'oeil fallen plant, 1989.
31. Decorative Arts, Inc., trompe l'oeil mural, 1992. Photo by Jimmy Prybill/Reflected Images.
32. Domenico Remps, attributed, *Cabinet of Curiosities*, c. late 17th century. Opificio delle Pietre Dure, Florence, Italy.
33. Carlo Crivelli, *Madonna and Child*, c. 15th century. The Metropolitan Museum of Art, The Jules Bache Collection, 1949. (49.7.5.) © 1984 by The Metropolitan Museum of Art.
34. Cy Twombly, *Untitled*, 1969, oil and crayon on canvas. Collection of Whitney Museum of American Art Purchase, with funds from Mr. and Mrs. Rudolph B. Schulhof, 69.29.
35. Wallerant Vaillant, *Letter Rack 1658*, 1658. Staatliche Kunstsammlungen, Dresden, Germany.
36. Samuel Lewis, *A Deception*, c. 1805-09. Private collection, photo courtesy of Kennedy Galleries, Inc., New York.
37. John Frederick Peto, *Card Rack with Jack of Hearts*, c. 1895. The Cleveland Museum of Art, Purchase from the J.H. Wade Fund.
38. John Frederick Peto, *Old Time Letter Rack*, 1894. Bequest of Maxim Karolik. Courtesy, Museum of Fine Arts, Boston.
39. William M. Harnett, *After the Hunt*, 1885. The Fine Arts Museums of San Francisco, Mildred Anna Williams Collection, 1940.93.
40. Anthony Fotia, trompe l'oeil mural, 1993.
41. Tromploy, Inc., trompe l'oeil faux sandstone room, 1987.
42. Shirley Pettibone, *Shore at Brighton Beach*, 1973.
43. Edwin Romanzo Elmer, *Magic Glasses*, 1891. Shelburne Museum, Shelburne, Vermont, Photograph by Ken Burris.
44. Baldassare Peruzzi, mural in the Villa Farnesina, Rome, Italy, 1515. Erich Lessing/Art Resource, New York.
45. Los Angeles Fine Arts Squad: Victor Henderson and Terry Schoonhoven, *Isle of California*, 1971. Courtesy of Koplin Gallery, Santa Monica, CA.
46. Richard Haas, mural, Thunderbird Fire and Safety Equipment Corp., Phoenix, Arizona, 1985.
47. Richard Haas, mural, Fountainebleau Hilton Hotel, Miami Beach, Florida, 1986.
48. Kent Addison, *Still Life #1019*, 1982.

Page 10, photo by Elaine Levin. Page 58, photo by Michael Dechillo, Gannett Westchester Newspapers.

INDEX